For my father

who taught me to see · H.T.

Copyright © 1998 Zero to Ten Ltd
Illustrations copyright © 1998 Hannah Tofts

Publisher: Anna McQuinn
Art Director: Tim Foster
Art Editor: Sarah Godwin
Designer: Suzy McGrath

This edition 1999
First published in Great Britain in 1998
by Zero to Ten Ltd
46 Chalvey Road East
Slough, Berkshire, SL1 2LR

A CIP catalogue record for this book
is available from the British Library.

ISBN 1-84089-118-1

Printed in Hong Kong

I Eat Vegetables!

Hannah Tofts

Photography by Rupert Horrox

Cabbage

Carrot

leaves

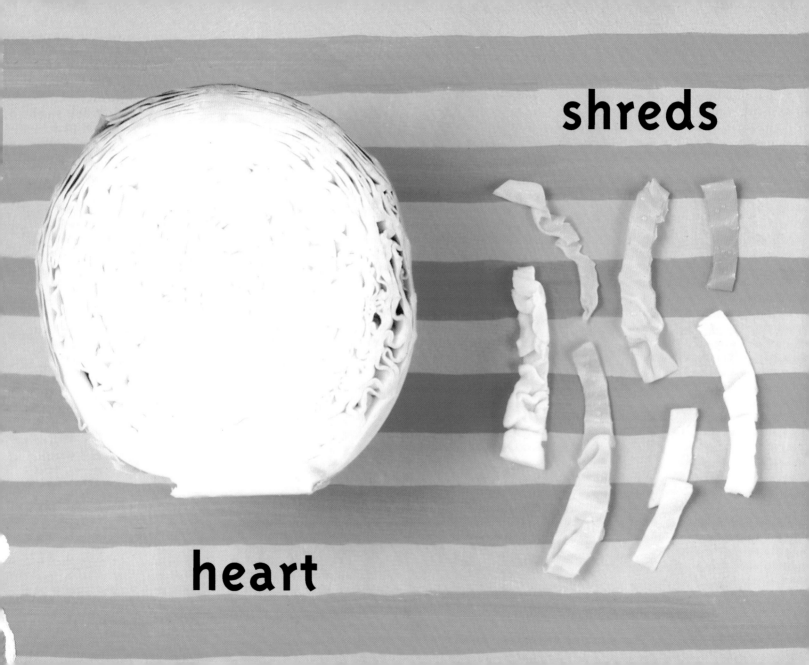

shreds

heart

Onion

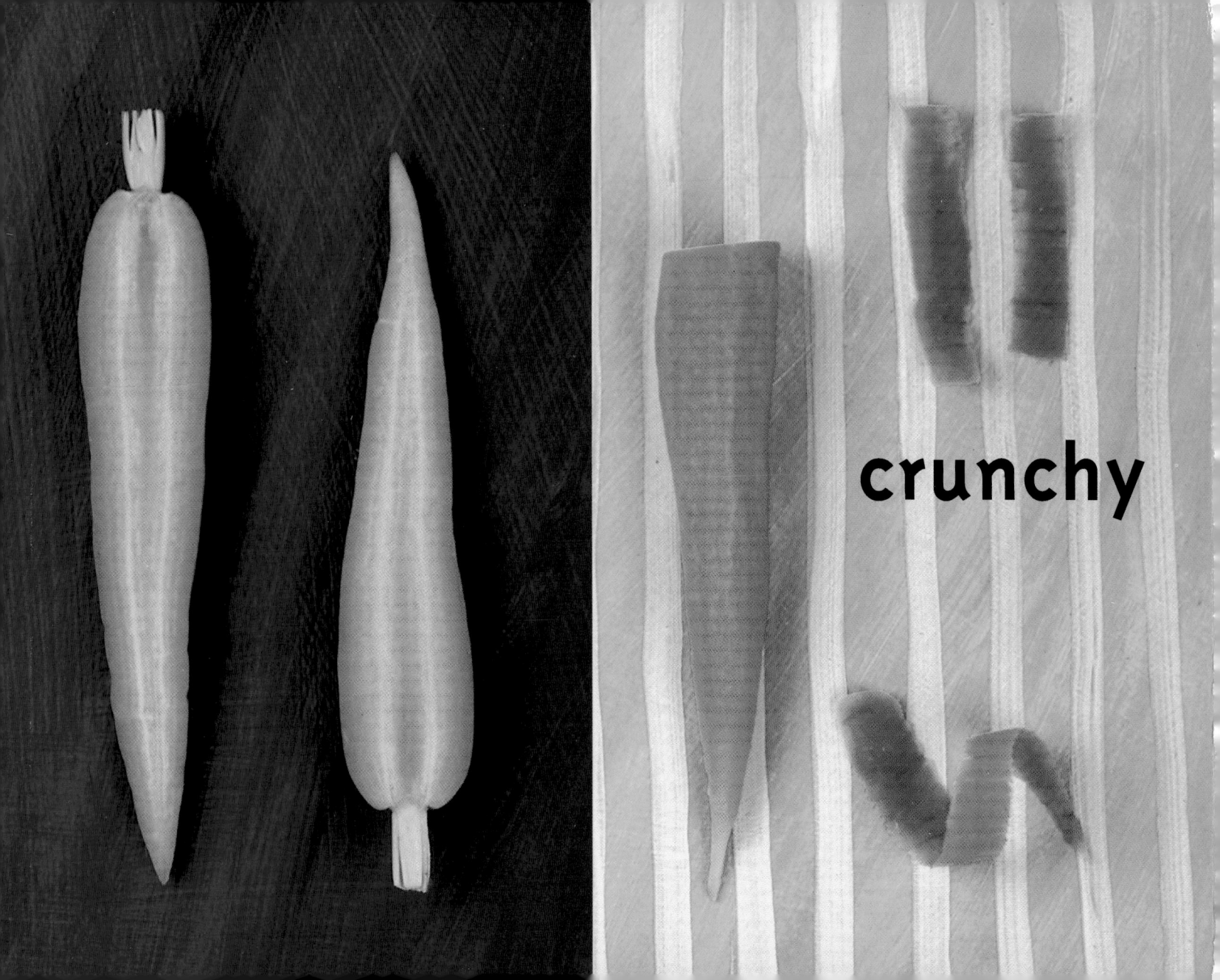

crunchy

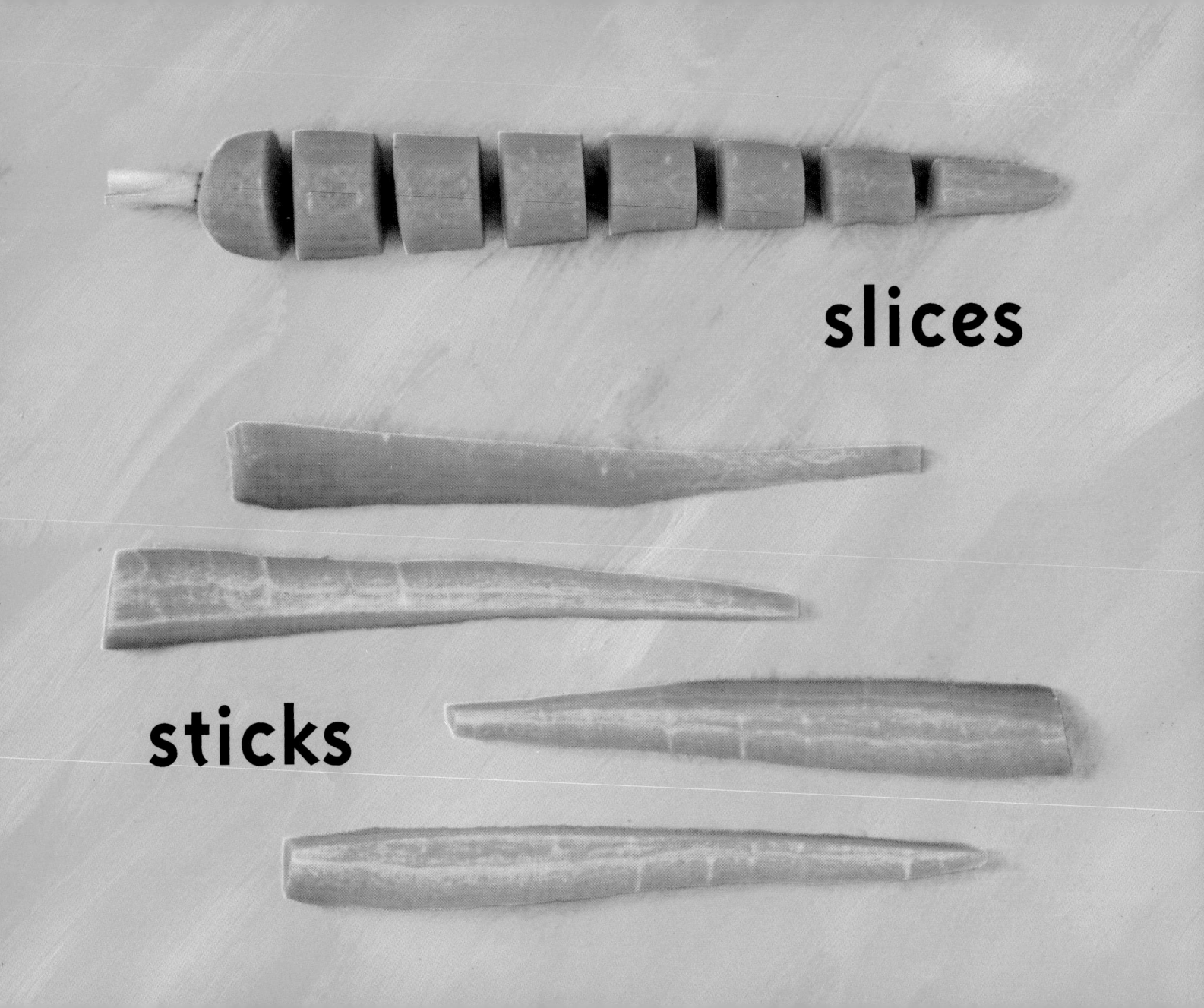

slices

sticks

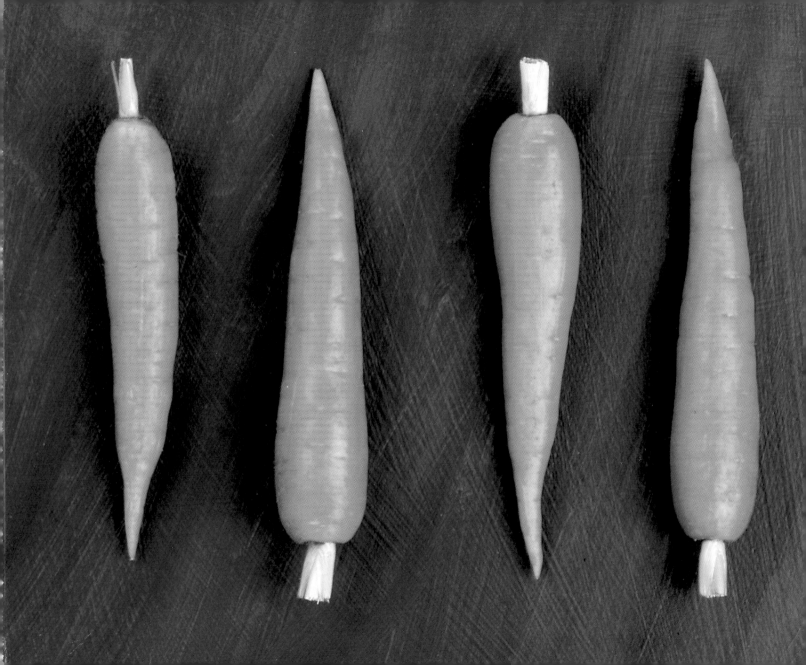

Corn

makes you cry

layers

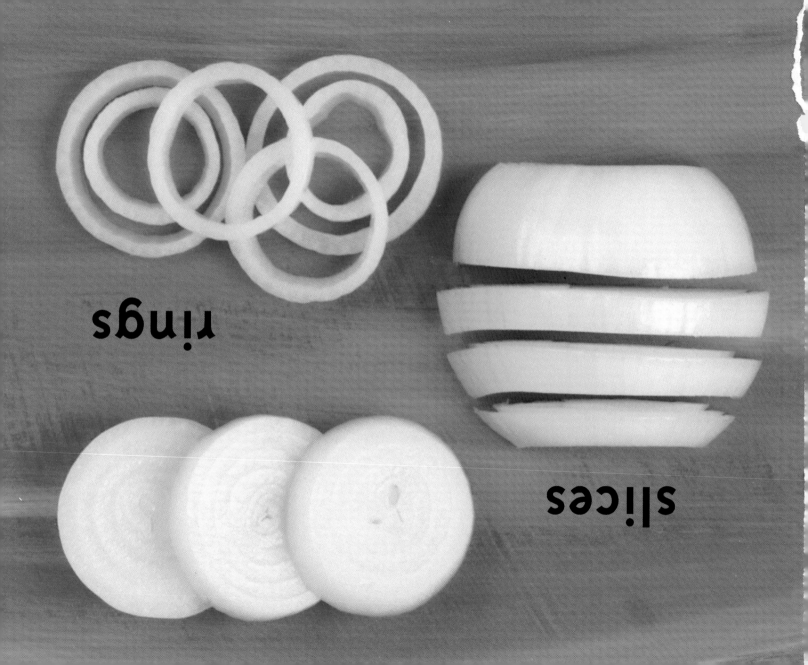

rings

slices

Tomato

corn-on-
the-cob

silky
hairs

kernels

Broccoli

slices

Peppers

stalk

head

florets

Potato

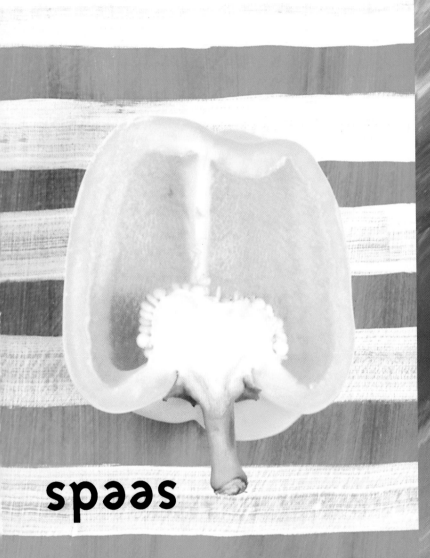

seeds

shiny skin

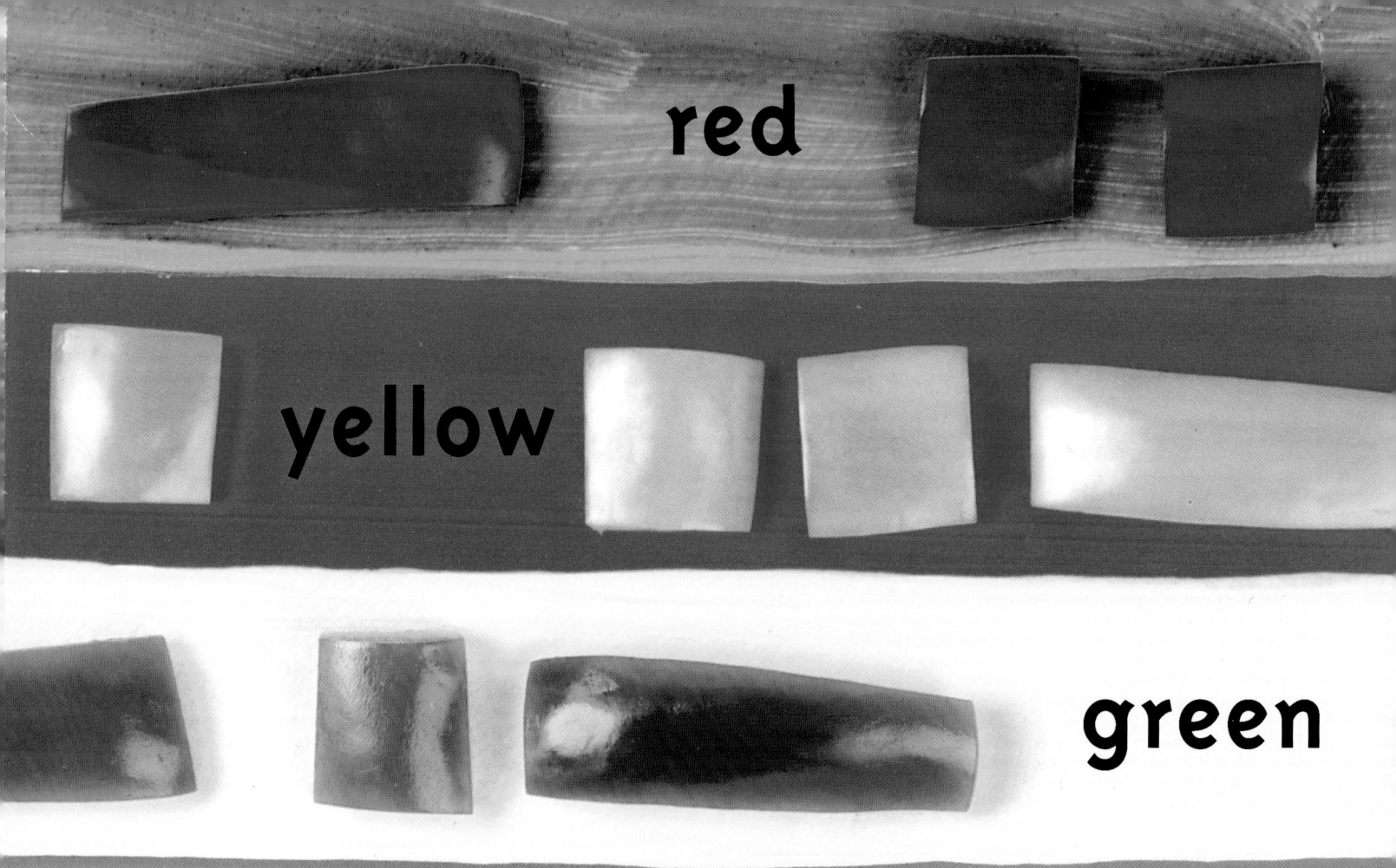

red

yellow

green

Which do you like to eat?

eyes

peel

halves